W9-BGJ-558

First Facts®

The Solar System

Earth

by Adele Richardson

Consultant:
Stephen J. Kortenkamp, PhD
Research Scientist
Planetary Science Institute, Tucson, Arizona

Capstone press®

Mankato, Minnesota

First Facts is published by Capstone Press,
151 Good Counsel Drive, P.O. Box 669, Mankato, Minnesota 56002.
www.capstonepress.com

Library of Congress Cataloging-in-Publication Data
Richardson, Adele, 1966–
    Earth / by Adele Richardson.—Rev. and updated.
    p. cm.—(First facts. The Solar system)
    Includes bibliographical references and index.
    ISBN-13: 978-1-4296-0720-9 (hardcover)
    ISBN-10: 1-4296-0720-3 (hardcover)
    1. Earth—Juvenile literature. I. Title. II. Series.
QB631.4.R52 2008
525—dc22   2007003526

Summary: Discusses the orbit, atmosphere, and surface features of Earth, and explains the
    conditions that make life possible on the planet.

Editorial Credits
Christopher Harbo, editor; Juliette Peters, designer and illustrator; Jo Miller, photo researcher;
    Scott Thoms, photo editor

Photo Credits
Bruce Coleman Inc./Jock Montgomery, 20
Digital Vision, 19
Image Ideas, 10
NASA, 16–17; Harrison H. Schmitt, 15
Photodisc, cover, 1, 4, 8, 9, 14, planet images within illustrations and chart 7, 11, 13, 21
Space Images/NASA/JPL, 5

1 2 3 4 5 6 12 11 10 09 08 07

Table of Contents

Galileo Flies By Earth

In 1989, the *Galileo* spacecraft began its trip through space. It flew by Venus once and Earth twice. Then it headed to Jupiter. As it passed Earth, scientists tested *Galileo's* cameras. The pictures showed a bright blue ball covered by clouds, water, and land.

Fast Facts about Earth

Diameter: 7,927 miles (12,757 kilometers)
Average Distance from Sun: 93 million miles (150 million kilometers)
Average Temperature: 60 degrees Fahrenheit (16 degrees Celsius)
Length of Rotation: 23 hours, 56 minutes
Length of Day: 24 hours
Length of Year: 365 days, 6 hours
Moons: 1

The Solar System

Earth is the third planet from the Sun. Mercury and Venus are closer, while Mars is farther away.
All four planets are made of rock. Jupiter, Saturn, Uranus, and Neptune are even farther from the Sun. These giant planets are made of gas and ice.

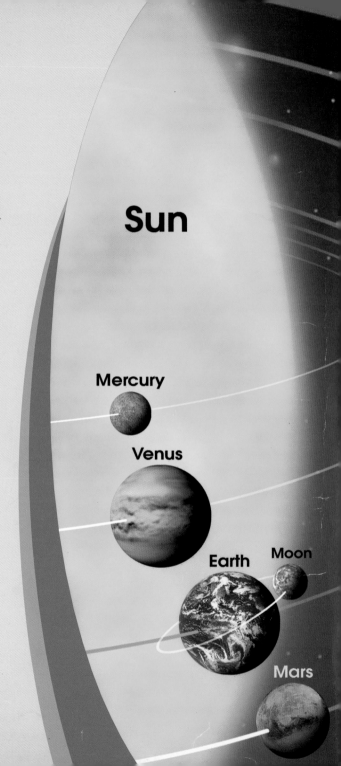

Sun

Mercury

Venus

Earth   Moon

Mars

Jupiter

Saturn

Uranus

Neptune

Earth's Atmosphere

The gases surrounding a planet are called its **atmosphere**. Earth's atmosphere is mostly made of **nitrogen** and **oxygen**.

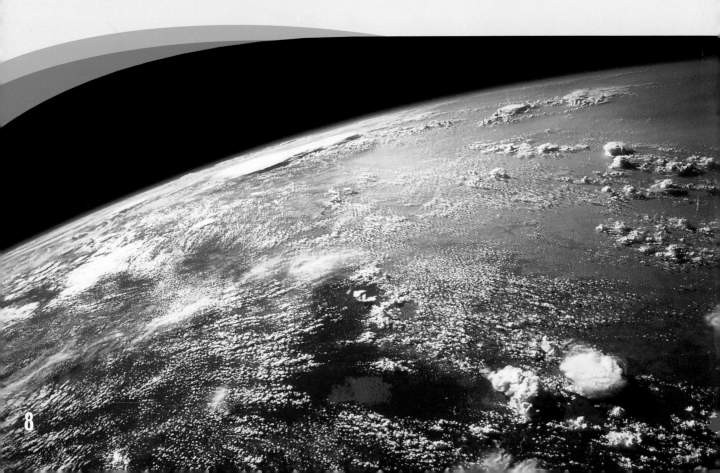

Earth's atmosphere keeps the planet warm. The atmosphere holds in heat from the Sun. Without the atmosphere, heat would escape into space.

Earth's Makeup

Earth is a rocky planet. Its surface, or crust, is solid rock. Water, mountains, and flat areas cover the crust. A **mantle** of melted rock lies below the crust.

Earth's center, or **core**, is made of two parts. The outer core is melted iron. The inner core is solid iron and nickel.

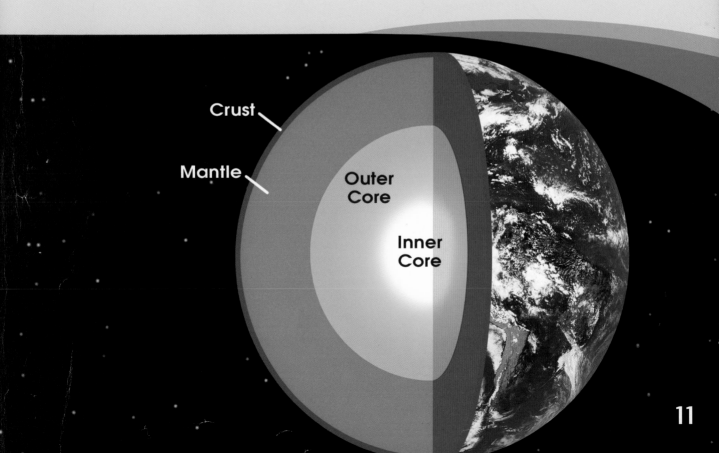

Crust

Mantle

Outer
Core

Inner
Core

How Earth Moves

Earth spins on its **axis** as it moves around the Sun. Earth takes almost 24 hours, or one day, to spin on its axis once. It takes Earth one year to circle the Sun. One year on Earth lasts 365 days and six hours.

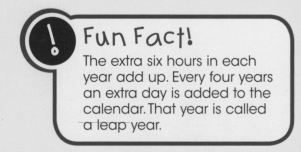

Fun Fact!
The extra six hours in each year add up. Every four years an extra day is added to the calendar. That year is called a leap year.

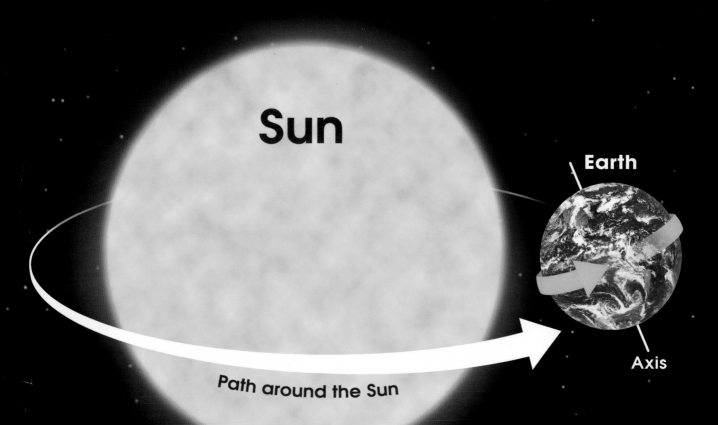

Sun

Earth

Axis

Path around the Sun

13

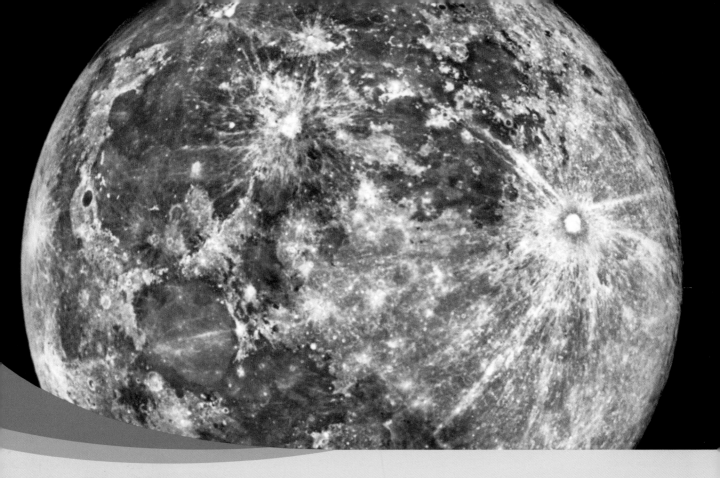

The Moon

Earth has one moon. The Moon is covered with rocks and dust. Its average distance from Earth is about 238,900 miles (384,500 kilometers).

Twelve people have walked on the Moon. It is the only body in space where people have landed.

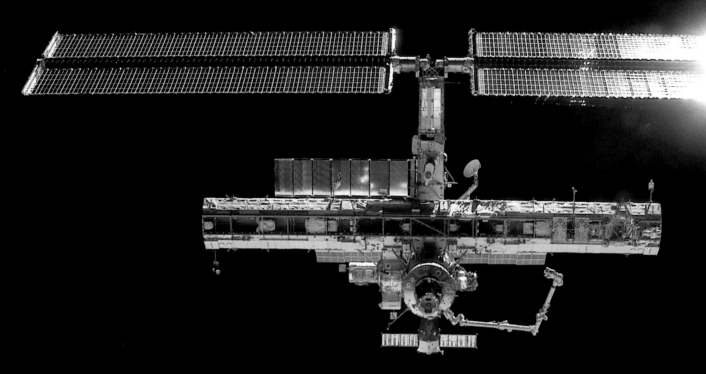

Studying Earth

Some scientists study Earth with **satellites.** Satellites are spacecraft that move around Earth. They take pictures of the planet's surface and atmosphere. Scientists also study Earth's mountains, oceans, and weather with satellites.

Fun Fact!
More than 70 percent of Earth is covered by water.

17

The Planet with Life

Earth is the only planet known to have life. Water and gases in the atmosphere allow life on the planet. The other planets are too hot or too cold. None of them have water on their surfaces or the right gases in their atmospheres. Only Earth has plants, animals, and people.

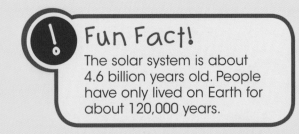

Fun Fact!

The solar system is about 4.6 billion years old. People have only lived on Earth for about 120,000 years.

Amazing but True!

Mount Everest is growing. Every year, it rises 2.5 inches (6 centimeters). How can this be? Earth's crust is made up of huge plates. These plates rub together and sometimes push rock upward. The plates moving under Mount Everest have made it the tallest mountain in the world.

Planet Comparison Chart

Planet	Size Rank (1=largest)	Makeup	1 Trip around the Sun (Earth Time)
Mercury	8	rock	88 days
Venus	6	rock	225 days
Earth	5	rock	365 days, 6 hours
Mars	7	rock	687 days
Jupiter	1	gases and ice	11 years, 11 months
Saturn	2	gases and ice	29 years, 6 months
Uranus	3	gases and ice	84 years
Neptune	4	gases and ice	164 years, 10 months

Glossary

atmosphere (AT-muhss-feehr)—the mixture of gases that surrounds some planets and moons

axis (AK-siss)—an imaginary line that runs through the middle of a planet; a planet spins on its axis.

core (KOR)—the inner part of a planet that is made of metal or rock

mantle (MAN-tuhl)—the part of a planet between the crust and the core

nitrogen (NYE-truh-juhn)—a colorless, odorless gas

oxygen (OK-suh-juhn)—a colorless gas in the air that people need to breathe

satellite (SAT-uh-lite)—a spacecraft that circles Earth; satellites take pictures and send messages to Earth.

Read More

Dunn, Mary R. *A Look at Earth.* Astronomy Now. New York: PowerKids Press, 2008.

Orme, Helen, and David Orme. *Let's Explore Earth.* Space Launch! Milwaukee: Gareth Stevens, 2007.

Taylor-Butler, Christine. *Earth.* Scholastic News Nonfiction Readers. New York: Children's Press, 2007.

Internet Sites

FactHound offers a safe, fun way to find Internet sites related to this book. All of the sites on FactHound have been researched by our staff.

Here's how:
1. Visit *www.facthound.com*
2. Choose your grade level.
3. Type in this book ID **1429607203** for age-appropriate sites. You may also browse subjects by clicking on letters, or by clicking on pictures and words.
4. Click on the **Fetch It** button.

FactHound will fetch the best sites for you!

Index